Self-Injury

When Pain Feels Good

Resources for Changing Lives

A Ministry of
THE CHRISTIAN COUNSELING AND
EDUCATIONAL FOUNDATION
Glenside, Pennsylvania

RCL Ministry Booklets
Susan Lutz, Series Editor

Self-Injury

When Pain Feels Good

Edward T. Welch

P&R PUBLISHING

P.O. BOX 817 • PHILLIPSBURG • NEW JERSEY 08865-0817

Printed in the United States of America

Library of Congress Cataloging-in-Publication Data

Welch, Edward T., 1953–
    Self-injury : when pain feels good / Edward T. Welch.
       p.cm.—(Resources for changing lives)
    Includes bibliographical references.
    ISBN 10: 0-87552-697-7
    ISBN 13: 978-0-87552-697-3
    1. Pastoral psychology. 2. Self-injurious behavior—
Religious aspects—Christianity. I. Title. II. Series.

BV4012.W38 2004
48.8'62—dc22

                           2004044152

If you have never purposely hurt yourself, it seems impossible to understand those who have. After all, don't living creatures *avoid* pain?

But if you *have* purposely hurt yourself, such behavior seems necessary, normal, even right. In fact, like a diabetic giving herself an injection, it can feel like a temporary cure.

This booklet assumes that you feel trapped in a cycle of intentional self-injury or that you love someone who does. Either you want help, or you want to give it. If you want to help, realize that cutting and similar behavior have their reasons. Begin trying to understand this person's world. If you are the one who feels trapped by the behavior, know that the cure is much more attractive than you think. Right now, you may hate your behavior, but you also feel like you need it. Self-injury might be your way to protect yourself from something worse. To give it up feels like a huge risk. And it would be—if you were left with no alternative. But there is a better way.

Anyone Feeling Alone?

No doubt you feel alone and isolated. You are reluctant to talk to people who want to help. When you do, they overreact. People just don't talk about purposeful self-injury anyway. No one uses it as a sermon illustration or mentions it in normal conversation. But though the behavior thrives on silence, those who self-injure number in the millions. Those who want to help number many more than that.

Fiona Apple, Garbage lead singer Shirley Manson, and actresses Angelina Jolie and Christina Ricci are a few celebrities who have acknowledged past problems with cutting. But this human experience has been around for a long time. The Bible describes ancient idol worshippers who "slashed themselves with swords and spears, as was their custom, until their blood flowed" (1 Kings 18:28). They believed this would appease their god. The practice even appeared in Christianity during the Middle Ages, when self-flagellation and other harmful practices were common forms of penance. They continue today in more private forms of self-denial.

There is little comfort in knowing you are not alone, but if other people have experienced it, maybe there is hope that you can be understood. If other people have helped, maybe you can help.

What Is It?

Self-injurers do various things. Nail biters don't stop until their fingers bleed. Pickers pick and scratch until they damage their skin or inflame old wounds. Cutters always have a razor blade handy to score, mark, or slash their body, which they then try to hide. Others punch themselves black and blue or burn themselves with cigarettes. Some break bones.

Anorexia, or purposeful starvation, is a form of self-injury that can accompany other forms or act as a gateway to further self-abuse. Men and women who severely restrict their diet are perfectionists who can never be perfect. They also try to hide from their feelings, which creates an environment in which cutting and hitting can thrive.

All this sounds like a death wish, and self-injurers *can* be suicidal, but there is a difference between the two behaviors. Those who purposefully cut an artery are trying to kill themselves. They want life to be over. Cutters tend to be more careful about where or how deeply they cut. They just want to feel better. Self-abusers typically want to live; they just don't know how to live with turbulent emotions.[1]

Slow Down: Consider Your Ways

If someone is in danger, we feel we must do something immediately, like stand guard over the person, or stop the cutter before something more serious happens. These responses are appropriate and usually driven by love. But you might have to go against your instincts with this. If you want to help but sense danger, talk with the self-abuser about your concerns. Self-injurers realize that you want to protect them, so be open with them. Ask about *their* assessment of the danger if you are concerned about suicide. If you need help, talk with a wise person who can help you make good decisions. In other words, slow down. There is a logic to the self-injurer's behavior and you must listen to it. Keep this in mind: the other person is more

---

1 Self-abuse should also be distinguished from an autistic person's head banging and other self-harming behaviors, as well a schizophrenic's response to directive, hallucinatory voices.

like you than you think. Beneath behavior that seems incomprehensible are familiar motivations—like fear, desire for control, hopelessness, sadness, anger.

If you are trapped in a self-injury cycle, you too must slow down. The cycle is becoming automatic. Your emotions tell you what to do and you robotically respond. Lies are becoming a way of life, distancing you from people who love you and might be able to help. Yes, slowing down can seem dangerous when your inner screams are getting louder and you feel that your only escape may soon be blocked. But there is another way. It is a path of wisdom, and wise people begin it by considering their ways.

The Cycle

The roots of the self-abuse cycle go deep, but it tends to be activated by "stress"—a difficult circumstance and your emotional response, or an intolerable emotional experience that no longer needs cues to trigger it. Common stressors are anger and frustration, anxiety, or a jumping-out-of-your-skin agitation. If you have no alternatives, self-injury gradually becomes the preferred response *because it works*. It provides an immediate sense of re-gained control and emotional relief. It offers a satisfying way to give voice to the silent screams within. In short, it brings peace; not lasting peace, but a crumb of calm or peace that is better than nothing. But when the experience of peace fades, the same circumstances and emotions are waiting to disrupt your inner world again, and the cycle continues, as the diagram shows.

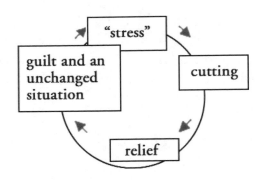

Why Self-Abuse? What Is the Behavior Saying?

It seems automatic, even instinctive, but there is a logic to self-inflicted pain. People do it for a reason. Even if the behavior is foreign to you, it isn't hard to think of some possible reasons for it. For example, if you hit someone, you are saying that you don't like him. You hit an enemy, someone who makes you angry. Might the same reasons apply to self-injury? Self-injurers can be angry at themselves. They can feel as if they have done something that deserves punishment. More specifically, they can feel like their bodies betrayed them. Perhaps a woman was sexually assaulted, and has started to believe, *My body is bad*. She reasons that if she'd had a male body, she wouldn't have been violated. Therefore, her female body is bad. Of course, the perpetrator is the real culprit, but you can see how this woman's self-injurious behavior has meaning and purpose for her.

This is only one possible reason. There are dozens of others, and self-injurious behavior can be saying more than one thing. Our feelings and behaviors can be dense with layers of meaning. Here is some of the reasoning behind self-injury.

"I am guilty. I must be punished."
This particular logic actually reveals keen insight—to a point. The biblical reality is that, before God, we all are guilty and deserve punishment. We have broken laws that reflect

God's character, so we have violated him. We follow our own desires rather than acknowledge that he is Lord. Some self-injurers even understand that shed blood is somehow the necessary penalty for guilt, as is demonstrated by their satisfaction when their cutting produces blood.

The problem is that this logic misses the deeper truth. When the Spirit of God reveals that we are guilty, he also reveals that *God himself provides the sacrifice*. In the Old Testament, the sacrifice was the blood of animals, but the people knew that this only offered a temporary cleansing. They had to shed this blood day after day, year after year. Thus the cutter is living like an Old Testament Hebrew who doesn't see that the sacrifices anticipate the Lamb of God. Jesus himself would take away the sins of the world once and for all.

"I am not perfect."

This is akin to guilt, but there is no obvious sin involved and God is not part of the picture. Here you have violated your own personal standards and desires. You didn't eat perfectly. You didn't look the way you wanted. The resulting feelings mimic guilt and, again, self-atoning blood seems like the only answer.

"They are right; I deserve this."

If self-injurers were sinned against by others, their behavior can be a way to agree with or approve of what was done to them: "Yes, you hurt me because I *deserve* to be hurt." Self-injurers hurt themselves before someone else can.

"I am angry."

Anger is frequently a message in self-injury. It can be a more aggressive way of saying, "I am guilty and deserve to be punished," but it often includes anger toward another person. Instead of hurting this person or taking the anger out on the family dog, the self-injurer hits him- or herself. "I hate you," is the refrain, but the focus of rage switches from self to others and back again.

"I can't feel this way any longer; hurting myself is the only way to stop my feelings."

When emotions seem overwhelming, you want them to stop. You *need* them to stop. Otherwise, they will kill you, drive you insane, or compel you to do something you desperately want to avoid. Self-injury temporarily relieves the pain, focuses your attention on the present, and leaves you feeling that you have regained control.

"I feel out of control (and other people have been in control). This way I can gain control (and no one can stop me)."

When self-injurers can find words, they often speak about "control."

"Words cannot express my pain."

Human beings usually put experience into language. Emotions need to be communicated. But what if there are no words? In that case, self-injury reflects a soul seeking expression. It may not be articulate or precise, but self-injury somehow captures the internal experience.

"Help!"

Some self-injurers want to keep their behavior a secret. It adds to the meaning of the ritual. But many want help and don't know how to ask. Perhaps they have never asked; perhaps they are too proud; perhaps they think no one cares enough to help.

If a person is hurting himself as a way to ask for help, it raises other questions. For example, why would you choose a private, harmful behavior to ask for something? Some spouses test their mates by wanting something from them without telling them what it is. They think, "If you love me, you will know without me telling you." If the spouse fails the test, the one who devised it feels justified in feeling rejected or angry. Here, self-injury can be used to justify self-pity and excessive self-concern.

This seems like a harsh way to explain the possible inner workings of self-injury, but if we really believe that self-injurers share a bond with those who *don't* purposely injure themselves, we would expect self-injurers to have a lot of "self" motivating their behavior. We all do! Scripture consistently reminds us that our greatest problem, even more than Satan himself, is our selfish desires (James 4:1–3). Pride and self-interest tend to rule our hearts. Contrary to what we may think, self-love is never a biblical command. The command is that we love others *to the degree* that we love ourselves (Matt. 19:18).

Identifying the purposes of self-injury is a useful step. Your emotions can be like a newborn baby who cries non-stop; when you understand the meaning behind the cries, you can help. In self-abuse, the cries are sometimes highly expressive, revealing the complexities of the human heart. Other times they are fairly simple: "I can't handle this feeling any more, and cutting eases the stress. If I don't cut myself, I will . . ." If this is all you understand about self-injury, you understand enough. There is a way out that will not destroy you.

Going Deeper: What Self-Abuse Is *Really* Saying

Now the critical point. Even though the knowledge of God might be nudged to the margins of our lives, everything we do is related to him, including self-injury. Self-injury is, at its root, about God. Avoid him, and we miss true hope.

"I am guilty" points to God.

It works this way. All our behavior says something about what we believe about God and our relationship with him. "I am guilty" is an obvious example. Guilt means that some standard has been violated. It could be a standard you set for yourself, your family's standard, or some vague cultural ideal. At first, it doesn't seem to have anything to do with God. But here is a given about human existence: what we see in ourselves and our relationships points to our deeper, though often avoided, relationship with God. If you hate people, you will find anger in your relationship with God. If you experience life as one oppressive standard, you will find a deeper sense that you don't measure up before

God and his standard, which is to love him with all your heart and to love your neighbor.

If you were OK before God—if somehow his standards could be met—wouldn't it make a difference with the other standards that leave you feeling like a failure? After all, God's standards are ultimately the ones that judge us, not our own or those of other people.

Here is where you will notice that you have serious misconceptions about God. God, you might think, is picky, never pleased, just waiting for you to blow it so he can rain punishment on you. Since he is going to do it, you might as well do it to yourself first. But the truth is that when God shows us that we don't measure up—and none of us do—this information is actually a sign of God's goodness to us. He is warning us that we are in mortal danger, walking a path more self-destructive than we think. Then he invites us back to him, where he is waiting to surprise us with the truth that we can find forgiveness in what Christ has done, rather than what we do. All we must do is believe.

To believe, of course, is not as easy as it sounds. To believe is to accept a lavish gift, and we are uneasy when we have nothing to give in return. We frantically look around for something to offer, such as our deep contrition or our self-loathing. This feels right at first, but it's not. A great gift calls attention to the generosity of the giver. It reminds us that we could not obtain the gift on our own. This means that any response to God's gift, other than thankfulness and praise, demeans the generosity of the giver and exaggerates our moral ability to contribute to the gift's cost. It means that we are looking at what *we* do rather than what God has done. God tells us to come to him with empty hands, but we want to wait until we feel more worthy. All the while, our Father in heaven keeps telling us that Jesus was worthy *for* us—we just need to trust him. He measured up because we never could.

Yes, it is hard to imagine that someone would love you enough to do this for you, but this is God's story. A sign that you are beginning to understand it is when you find it too good to be true. If you hear the story as a tale of condemnation and a life of trying harder to measure up, you are putting your own twist on it. Your story is about your failure. God's story is about how, when you trust in Jesus, his story becomes your own.

"I am angry" points to God.
Here is what "I am angry" can say:

"I am angry, and I am ultimately angry with God. He could have made things different than they are."

"You [another person] are wrong. I am right. I judge you and find you guilty. And I am going to mete out the punishment because I don't believe that God is a good judge. I don't trust him to administer the justice I think I deserve."

"If I am going to be judged and feel guilty, then I am going to judge others too. I don't believe that God shows mercy to me, so I won't show it to others."

Once again, these statements take us back to the true story that God tells us rather than the one we tell ourselves.

God is in control.

We can trust that he is the righteous judge of all the world.

For those who trust him, all his judgment has fallen on Jesus Christ.

He is the God who loves to show mercy and extend forgiveness.

Put the Silence into Speech

Even the simple and desperate cry, "I can't feel this way any longer; hurting myself is the only way to stop the feelings," is about God. At first glance this too seems unrelated to him—and that is just the point. When we cry, but *not* to the One who hears us, we are saying that God doesn't hear, care, or love.

Children who are hurt run to a parent who will listen and show compassion. As creatures in relationships, we share our pain with those who love us. If we do this with people like ourselves—imperfect lovers who are rarely powerful enough to do anything—how much more should we cry out to our heavenly Father, who loves perfectly and responds to our cries?

When his people experienced trouble, the Lord said, "They do not cry out to me from their hearts but wail upon their beds. . . . They do not turn to the Most High; they are like a faulty bow" (Hos. 7:14, 16).

God is talking about people who are hurting, inviting them to turn to him, but they prefer the isolation of crying on their beds. This self-oriented posture pervades history. In our misery we are simply not inclined to turn to the Lord. As a result, human history and our individual stories are cycles of turning toward the Lord and turning away from him. "Then they cried to the LORD in their trouble, and he saved them from their distress," is the recurring chorus of the Hebrew people (Ps. 107:19). Our wandering hearts don't turn once to the Lord. They stray and then return to him over and over.

One reason we would rather turn to another human being is that there are fewer strings attached: we call out; they listen. But when we turn to the Lord, our fundamental allegiances change: we call out, he listens and acts, we follow him. Turning to the Lord leads to our very lives finding residence in Jesus Christ. For people who want personal control and independence, as some self-injurers do, this is too high a price. But even then the Lord invites us.

The invitation comes with a promise: "For the LORD will not reject his people" (Ps. 94:14). If you feel as though you are not good enough to come to Christ, you have met the standard for coming! The invitation goes to people who feel like they can't measure up. But if you feel as though you are worse than the worst, be careful. You might be minimizing the love that Jesus has already demonstrated by suggesting that God's love has human-like limits. You might be making a religious-sounding excuse that gives you a clear conscience about avoiding Jesus. If you reject an invitation to a wonderful party by saying you aren't worthy, very likely you just did not want to go.

Cries of the Heart

Let's assume that, on some level, you are reluctant to turn to the Lord with your pain. You aren't willing to give up the behavior that seems to work for you. Even if this is how you feel, Jesus speaks words of grace to you.

When you have experiences that are hard to put into words, it helps when someone can identify with them without needing you to explain them. You feel blessed, more hopeful, and less isolated. This is what the Lord does. As he invites us to turn to him, he describes our experience. When we don't have the words, he speaks them for us and invites us to join in. You find these words in the Psalms. If you read them, it will be like hearing your own soul speak.

"Answer me when I call to you, O my righteous God. Give me relief from my distress; be merciful to me and hear my prayer." (Ps. 4:1)

"Give ear to my words, O LORD, consider my sighing. Listen to my cry for help, my King and my God, for to you I pray." (Ps. 5:1–2)

"My soul is in anguish. How long, O LORD, how long?" (Ps. 6:3)

"O God, you are my God, earnestly I seek you; my soul thirsts for you, my body longs for you, in a dry and weary land where there is no water." (Ps. 63:1)

Why did God include psalms in the Bible? Certainly, they teach us how to worship the Lord, but there is more. Do you notice that God actually wants us to speak to him when we struggle, so much so that when we are speechless, he offers us words to say? In one psalm after another, he invites us to cry out to him rather than cry on our beds.

With this in mind, find a psalm to call your own, one that captures your experience and turns you to the Lord rather than to self-injury. Start with phrases or sections of the psalm and speak them from your heart to the Lord. Don't forget that these words are not simply those of a human poet expressing his sorrow or isolation. They are divinely authorized words; Jesus himself used many of them to call out to his Father. They teach us how to call out to the God who delights to hear us.

Words of Confession

Once we get used to calling out to the Lord, more words are available to us. Some of the most important are words of confession.

Confession of sin, admittedly, has a bad reputation. It evokes images of punishment, shame, and someone's anger against us. But the reality is that we all sin every day, and conviction of sin is evidence that God's Spirit is working in our lives. Sin is against God, but an awareness of sin is a gift *from* God. So include words of confession when you speak to God.

The goal is not to come up with a long list of individual sins. The goal is to confess that your sinful behavior and thoughts were *against God*. For example, selfishness is sin because life is not about us; it's about the glory of God. Gossip is sin because it speaks against people created in God's image. Everyone can acknowledge that they do wrong things sometimes. Many can admit they are sinners. But it is less common to remember that sin is against God. Scripture even says that the ordinary conflicts of life are actually evidence of hatred against God (James 4:4).

Our confessions might sound something like this: "Father, I confess that, in hurting myself, I ignore that you were wounded for me. I am doubting your promises, even though I know that you speak truth."

"Father, I confess that I prefer to turn inward than to turn to you. Yet I am so over-whelmed by the things I feel. Please help me."

"Father, I confess that I do this because I want to control rather than trust in your control."

The freedom to confess comes from knowing that, through Jesus Christ, "where sin increased, grace increased all the more" (Rom. 5:20). No matter how much sin we discover in ourselves, there is more than enough grace and mercy to forgive and change us. God takes joy in forgiving us. It makes his name great to offer forgiveness that goes beyond anything in human relationships.

After confession, Scripture gives us more words to say. "If you, O LORD, kept a record of sins, O LORD, who could stand? But with you there is forgiveness" (Ps. 130:3–4). Be sure to end with thanks, not guilt!

Shame, Memories, and Victimization

Forgiveness is our deepest need. It goes to the depths of the struggle with self-injury. But forgiveness doesn't always connect as clearly with the shame that can motivate self-injury.

Failure

Shame comes in several forms. Sometimes we feel like we haven't measured up to our own or others' ideals. We aren't pretty enough, we didn't achieve enough, we feel below average generally, or we go unnoticed by important people. These can be deep hurts that self-injury can express. It can also be a way to punish ourselves for not being better than we are. Such self-injury is a way to cling to the idea that we are unique.

Some of these struggles with shame can be responded to with simple wisdom. For example, if you want to hurt yourself because you did poorly on an exam, decide instead to learn from your mistakes, ask for help, and prepare well for the next one.

But if you feel that other people will be smarter no matter what you do, what are you saying about your relationship with God? Sometimes self-loathing is rooted in pride, although it certainly doesn't feel that way! On the surface, the problem seems to be just the opposite—that we need to think better of ourselves. But if you search your heart for pride, it is usually there in some form.

In this case the pride is evident in the way we want more *for ourselves*. We want to be great in something. We want recognition, reputation—some kind of personal glory—and we aren't getting it. We want it more than we want God. We want to be a god rather than trust the true God.

What's the alternative? We confess what's going on and turn to the God whose glory and holiness leave us in awe, and whose humility leaves us with a different model of true humanness.

Dashed Hopes and Rejection

Another kind of shame comes when we have been rejected by someone significant. Perhaps a boyfriend sinned against you; perhaps you wanted a relationship that he didn't. Since rejection can trigger a compulsion to self-injure, this is a time to slow down. Call out to the Lord, don't cry on your bed. Face your doubts about God's plans for your life. Right now it feels like misery, but if God sent Jesus to die so we could live, why would he be uncaring now? God's plans include hardship and disappointment, but his love has already been proven in Jesus, and it is more sophisticated than we know. Even in our hardship he is doing good. Sometimes the good is teaching us to trust him. It is a spiritual response with eternal value.

Victimization

The most profound kind of shame comes when we have been physically or sexually violated. The language of self-abuse has multiple layers, expressing anger, self-loathing, pain, guilt, and self-punishment. With so much inside, victims feel like it is the only way to get temporary relief.

Victims can find words to express their pain in the Psalms. So often they are the cries of the innocent and oppressed. But God's words to the victimized go beyond the Psalms. The entire Bible speaks comfort and encouragement to those who have known injustice.

"Woe," the Lord says, "to the shepherds who only take care of themselves. You have ruled [my people] harshly and brutally. Therefore, I am against the shepherds and will hold them accountable for my flock" (see Ezek. 34:2–10). Then the Lord searches for his flock, rescues them, and leads them personally to rich pastures.

The prophet Isaiah anticipated a time when there would be no more shame. He addressed the women who suffered the most shame in his day. "Sing, O barren woman. . . . Do not be afraid; you will not suffer shame. Do not fear disgrace; you will not be humiliated. You will forget the shame of your youth. . . . For your Maker is your husband—the LORD Almighty is his name—the Holy One of Israel is your Redeemer" (Isa. 54:1–6). In Christ, this time has come.

The Road Leads to Jesus

Isaiah points us to the true destination. Crying out to God, confessing sin, and trusting his character are critical steps that all lead to Jesus. Jesus is the focal point of all Scripture, and true hope can be found when we pursue the same goal.

Isaiah could announce this blessing because he had prophetically witnessed the sufferings and resurrection of Jesus (Isa. 53). He saw that one man would be rejected, shamed, victimized, and crushed for our sins so that his offspring could prosper. We are his offspring if we turn to him.

We still have a tendency to draw a sharp distinction between the wrath of God and the love of Jesus. But Jesus is the full expression— "the exact representation" (Heb.1:3)—of God's being. If we see and know Jesus, we see and know the Father; they are one. The cross reveals God's anger with sin *and* his love for his people. It reveals Jesus' humility to serve even to death *and* his greatness, power, and exaltation since death has no power over him.

You want to find home. You want peace and rest. You have looked for these things when you hurt yourself, but having control is not all it's cracked up to be. Now, look away from yourself. The answers reside in Jesus. Seek him and he will be found.

Action Steps

After reading about the big picture, here are some specific steps you can take.

1. Do you want to change? The usual answer is "yes" *and* "no." Change is hard, in part because we don't want to change. Our behavior creates inconveniences, but it still serves a purpose in our lives. So ask this question regularly. It will remind you to confront your motivations and bring them to the Lord. It takes time to realize that the path with Jesus is better than the path of self-injury.

2. Allow other people in. Self-injury likes privacy but God's path is one of light and openness. If you don't speak openly and honestly to someone you trust and who can help, it probably means that you aren't yet willing to change.

3. Grow in honesty. Lies come in many forms, from whoppers to silent cover-ups. Every day, think about how you have tried to hide your behavior. Confess these things to God and consider confessing to the person you misled. When lies pile up in relationships, we feel more shame, isolation, and hopelessness. It is one of the Devil's favorite strategies.

4. Feed yourself with Scripture. Psalms, a Gospel, and Ephesians are good places to start. Journaling can help you meditate on Scripture.

5. Find good books that communicate clearly about God's grace. Consider *The Cross-Centered Life* by C. J. Mahaney or other books available through Resources for Changing Lives.

6. Since your self-injury follows a pattern in which you can anticipate the situations, times, and places when you are most vulnerable, what alternative plans can you make when those situations arise? Remember, you must choose these alternatives (calling a friend, reading at a public place) long before your emotions reach their crisis point.

7. Write out the meaning and purpose of your self-injury. What are you saying by it?

8. When you blow it, don't give in to hopelessness. All human beings blow it. It is what we do! But when we turn to Jesus and receive his Spirit, nothing is hopeless. We have forgiveness, deeper wisdom, and power to walk another path. If you are stuck in hopelessness, is it because you *want* to stay stuck?

9. Search the Psalms to give voice to your heart and pattern your personal reflections after them: they are honest, not always pretty, yet consistently end with praise and thanks.

Edward T. Welch directs the School of Biblical Counseling at the Christian Counseling and Educational Foundation, where is he a counselor and faculty member.

RCL Ministry Booklets